Pebble Plus

Stephen Harper

by Jennifer Sutoski

CAPSTONE PRESS
a capstone imprint

Pebble Plus is published by Capstone Press,
1710 Roe Crest Drive, North Mankato, Minnesota 56003
www.capstonepub.com

Library of Congress Cataloging-in-Publication Data
Cataloging-in-publication information is on file with the Library of Congress.

ISBN 978-1-4914-7833-2 (library binding : alk. paper)
ISBN 978-1-4914-7841-7 (pbk. : alk. paper)
ISBN 978-1-4914-7856-1 (eBook PDF)

Developed and Produced by Discovery Books Limited
Paul Humphrey: project manager
Sabrina Crewe: editor
Ian Winton: designer

Photo Credits
Mykhaylo Palinchak/Shutterstock: cover, 19; Intoit/Shutterstock: title page; Andy Clark/Reuters/Corbis: 5; Image courtesy of the University of Calgary Archives (UARC 2001.066_ph4.15_4): 7 top left; Jeff Whyte/Shutterstock: 7 (right); Courtesy of Richview Collegiate: 7 (bottom left); Image courtesy of the University of Calgary Archives (UARC 2001.066_ph5.15_6): 9; Todd Korol/Reuters/Corbis: 11; Shaun Best/Reuters/Corbis: 13; National Capital Commission: 15 (top); Martin Good/Shutterstock: 15 (bottom); Chris Wattie/Reuters/Corbis: 17; Wu Wei/Xinhua Press/Corbis: 21.

Note to Parents and Teachers

The Canadian Biographies set supports national curriculum standards for social studies related to people and culture. This book describes and illustrates Stephen Harper. The images support early readers in understanding text. The repetition of words and phrases helps early readers learn new words. This book also introduces early readers to subject-specific vocabulary words, which are defined in the Glossary section. Early readers may need assistance to read some words and to use the Table of Contents, Glossary, Read More, Internet Sites, and Index sections of the book.

Printed in China through World Print Ltd in 2015
007326WPF15

Table of Contents

Early Years

Stephen Joseph Harper was born April 30, 1959, in Toronto, Ontario. He is the oldest of three brothers in the Harper family.

born in Toronto

1959

Stephen Harper visits the house in Toronto where he grew up.

Stephen Harper worked hard at school in Toronto. At university, he became interested in politics. He helped start a political party. The Reform Party wanted to change people's ideas about how to run Canada.

born in Toronto

1959

1987

helps start Reform Party

Stephen Harper's high school

Stephen Harper went to the University of Calgary.

Making a speech for the Reform Party

A Career and Family

Stephen Harper became a full-time politician. In 1993, he was elected to be a Member of Parliament (MP) for Calgary. MPs come to Parliament from all over the country. They make laws for Canada.

Stephen Harper (right) in Parliament with other Reform Party MPs

Also in 1993, Stephen Harper married Laureen Teskey. In 1996, the Harpers had a son, Benjamin. Three years later, their daughter Rachel was born.

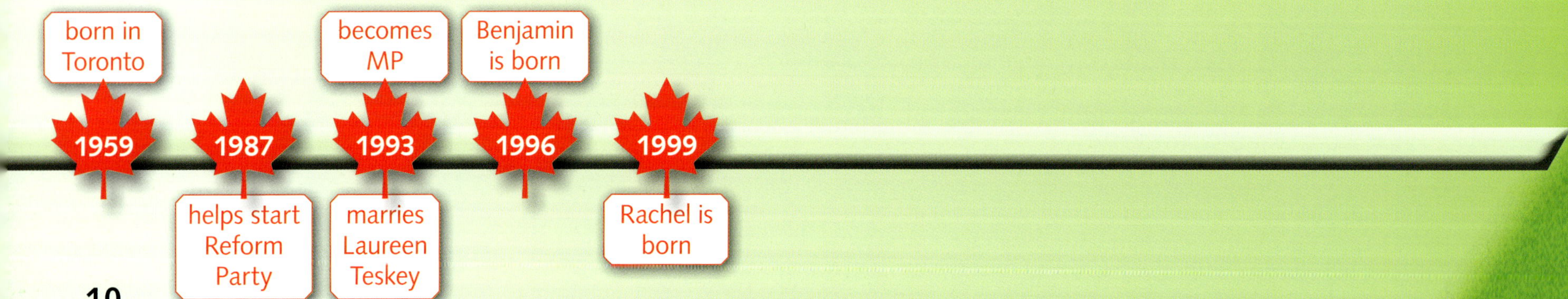

The Harper family at the Calgary Stampede in 2007

In 2002, Stephen Harper became leader of a party called the Canadian Alliance. Then his party joined with another party to become the Conservative Party. Stephen Harper became its leader in 2004.

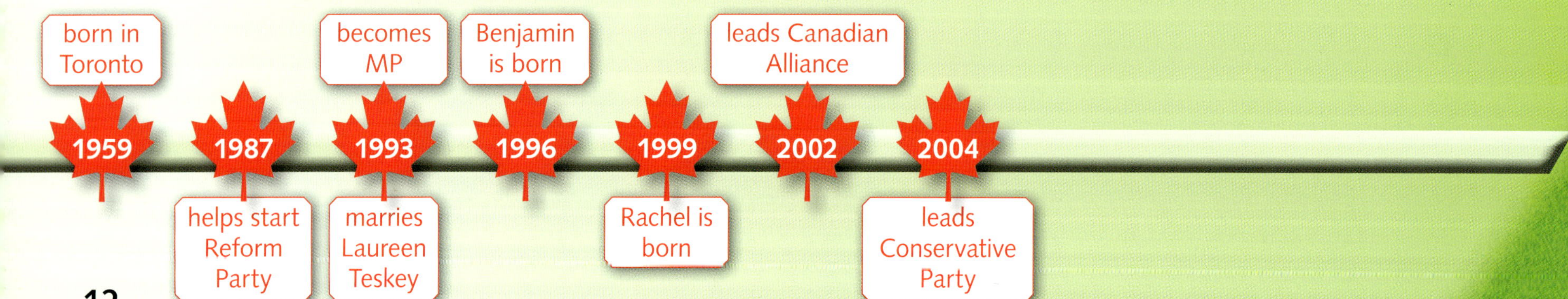

Stephen Harper wins the Conservative Party leadership.

Prime Minister

The Conservative Party came to power in 2006. Stephen Harper became the Prime Minister. He moved with Laureen, Benjamin, and Rachel to a house in Ottawa kept for prime ministers' families.

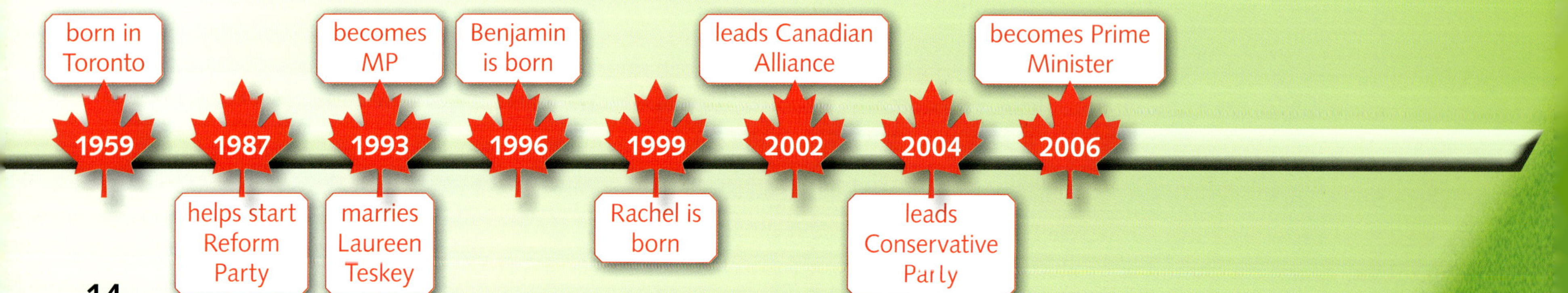

The Harpers live at 24 Sussex Drive, Ottawa, Ontario.

The Prime Minister works at the Houses of Parliament.

Stephen Harper was elected again in 2008 and 2011. The Prime Minister is Canada's most powerful politician. He is leader of the government. He makes decisions for the whole country.

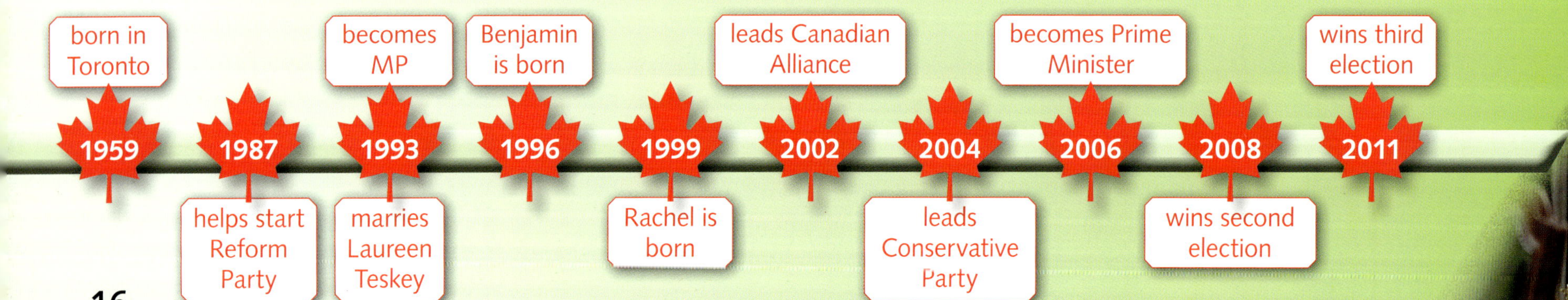

Stephen Harper speaking in Parliament

Canada's Prime Minister represents our country all over the world. Stephen Harper goes to meetings with other world leaders. He invites foreign leaders to visit Canada.

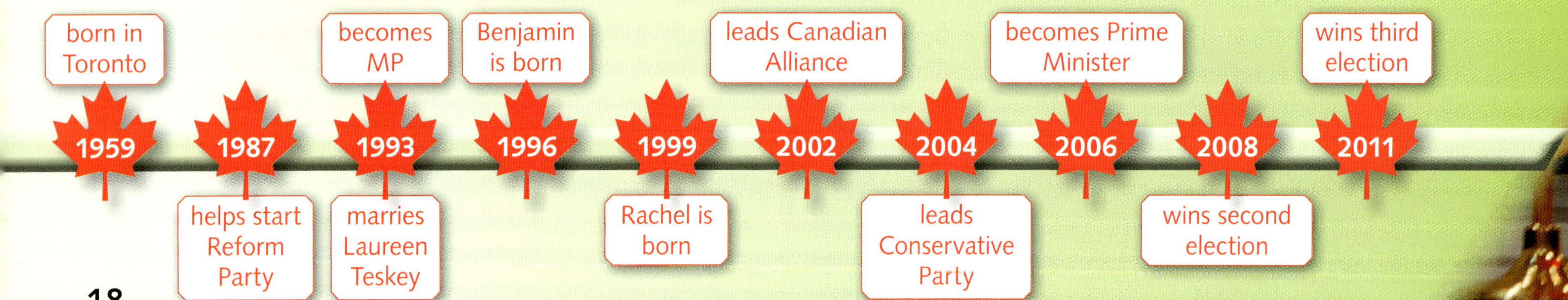

President Petro Poroshenko from Ukraine visits Prime Minister Harper.

A Proud Canadian

Stephen Harper enjoys ice hockey. He wrote a book about the history of hockey. Stephen Harper is not just the leader of Canada. He is also a proud Canadian.

- **1959** born in Toronto
- **1987** helps start Reform Party
- **1993** becomes MP
- **1993** marries Laureen Teskey
- **1996** Benjamin is born
- **1999** Rachel is born
- **2002** leads Canadian Alliance
- **2004** leads Conservative Party
- **2006** becomes Prime Minister
- **2008** wins second election
- **2011** wins third election

Stephen Harper at a hockey game in Vancouver

Glossary

elect—to pick one person from a group by voting

government—the group in charge of running a country

law—a rule that all Canadians must follow

MP—stands for Member of Parliament, a person elected to make laws

Parliament—the place where people make laws, and the name of the group that makes them

political party—a group of people who share ideas about how to run the country

politician—a person involved in government or elections

politics—anything to do with government and electing people to government

prime minister—the leader of the government

represent—to act for other people by making decisions on their behalf or speaking for them

Read More

Rodger, Ellen. *How Does the Canadian Government Work?* St. Catharines, ON: Crabtree, 2013.

Internet Sites

FactHound offers a safe, fun way to find Internet sites related to this book. All of the sites on FactHound have been researched by our staff.

Here's all you do:

Visit *www.facthound.com*

Type in this code: 9781491478332

Index

Word Count: 262

Grade: 1

Early-Intervention Level: 17